Thy

Kingdom

Come

By

Dr. James Wilkins

Finally, Peace Comes to the Earth

THY KINGDOM COME
Finally, Peace Comes To The Earth

New Testament Ministries
Dr. James Wilkins, Director
P.O. Box 291
Bedford, TX 76095
Pwilkins96@sbcglobal.net

Creative services and printing through:
CSN Books Publishing
1975 Janich Ranch Court
El Cajon, CA 92019-1150
Toll Free: 1-866-484-6184
CSNbooks.com

All Scripture taken from the King James Version of the Bible.

Printed in the United States of America.

TABLE OF CONTENTS

THY KINGDOM COME

The next dispensation, which follows our present age, is **the millennial reign of Christ**. We could be in that glorious age before the fellow that bought that luxurious new SUV today has it paid off. He was placed on the **seven-year** payment plan because of his good credit record.

When Jesus comes back as a thief in the night to rapture His saints, the saved will go to the Judgment Seat of Christ and to the great rewards banquet. On earth, the Great Tribulation will begin and the last half of the seven-year period will be so horrible that no flesh will survive, except those days be shortened. That's right, no flesh or human being will survive all of the catastrophes that will conclude with the Battle of Armageddon, **unless those days** (seven years) shall be shortened (*Matt. 24:22)*.

I. IT IS TIME TO START THINKING ABOUT THE KINGDOM

There are at least four reasons why you should begin to think about the coming 1000-year reign:

1. Time Could Be Very Short.

It may not be in seven years, but then again, it could be. We don't know. In fact, no one knows the day and hour of His return except God, the Father. Nor do we know what position we will hold in the millennial Kingdom. This statement is directed to the saved only, because a non-Christian has a very small chance of ever escaping the Tribulation and seeing the millennium. **Anything with the potential of being so sudden** and dramatic should occupy your mind and concern.

2. Upon Graduation You Will Move There.

Death is described as a graduation for the child of God. Death, to the child of God, is the servant who ushers him into the presence of God in Heaven. Since we move from time into **a land that is eternal**, it is my opinion that it will seem but a very short amount of time before we go to the Bema Stand (Judgment Seat of Christ) and then into the millennium. **Your graduation could happen before** the fellow with the good credit record makes his first payment, or his last. We have no assurance of how long we will live. But we know that, *"It is appointed unto men once to die, but after this the judgment" (Heb. 9:27).*

3. You Will Live There 1000 Years.

An old Gospel song pictures someone standing on Jordan's stormy banks (death) and casting a wishful eye. He is looking, according to the song, to Canaan Land (Heaven) where his possessions lie.

Think with me about this. Death divides your present life from your future life. You have a few years on this side of death, and **1000 years on the other side of death**. It will be at least 1000 years before you will go **into eternal Heaven**, where you will not have a vivid memory of your present life with its deeds and misdeeds. Your memory will be changed **after** the Great White Throne of Judgment (for the lost), which will happen at the end of millennium (*Rev. 20:1-12).* God will then create a new Heaven and a new earth. When this happens, **He will wipe all tears away** and, *"the former things are passed away" (Rev. 21:4).* Until that happens, our memories will live with **the commendation or rebuke** that Jesus gives us at the Judgment Seat.

The law of big numbers, which the insurance companies use to compute mortality tables, says that a man of average health will live approximately 82.4 years. Your writer is, as of this writing, 73.6 years old. Using their numbers and "the river" as a symbol of death, he has a little less than nine years **on this side** of death. According to the Bible, he has 1000 years to live **on the other side** of the river.

4. What Job Should You Worry About?

What makes more sense – worrying about this short journey to the river or a long-term career on the other side of the river? God has already promised (in *Matt. 6:33)* that if one will seek first the Kingdom of God, then He will supply all his needs. Your Heavenly Father has promised to help you as you serve **as the steward over your short life on this earth**. He even stated that it is His (God's) good pleasure to aid and help you while you labor to fulfill your purpose.

But your Papa, our Heavenly Father, the mighty Creator of Heaven and earth, really wants you to have a good position for the complete 1000-year reign when His Son, Jesus, is the world's boss. Remember, what you do during this short stay on the earth **will determine** where you will live and what you will be doing for the full 1000 years.

II. THE PROMINENCE OF THE KINGDOM

The question, "What position will you occupy in His Kingdom?" **startles people, but it shouldn't**. It was something the early Christians thought about. Two of the apostles even sent their mother to request that they might sit on either side of Jesus during His 1000-year reign. Their request caused great dissension and brought rebuke from Jesus, but it shows that early followers of Jesus were already thinking about the soon-coming Kingdom.

1. Pray For The Kingdom To Come.

Not only did the disciples think about the coming 1000-year reign, but Jesus taught them, and all Christians, to pray for the coming Kingdom.

"Thy kingdom come. Thy will be done in earth, as it is in Heaven" (Matt. 6:100. The smallest little Sunday school child recognizes

that expression as one which is found in the Lord's (model) prayer. It is probably one of the first prayers a child is taught to pray. *"Our Father, which art in Heaven, hallowed be thy name.* ***Thy kingdom come...*** *" (Matt. 6:9-13).*

That is not just a beautiful little saying that sounds good, but it is a command by our Savior to pray for His soon coming Kingdom. He knew that if we prayed for the coming Kingdom, we would have the possibility of living our lives **in the light of that coming and eternity**. We would live our lives focused on the coming world instead of being so involved in the present world all around us, which will soon pass away.

2. Look Toward The Kingdom To Come.

The very first sermon Jesus preached was about the coming Kingdom, *"Repent: for the kingdom of heaven is at hand" (Matt. 4:17).*

For the first three years of His ministry, He offered the literal Kingdom to Israel. He did everything to prove to the Jews that He was their promised Messiah. The Jews marveled at His knowledge and the power of His preaching as He used the Scriptures to prove that He was "the great **I AM**" and their coming Messiah.

His miracles proved He was the supernatural God who had come to the earth wrapped in human flesh. Although the common man was convinced, the Jewish leaders refused to accept these infallible miracles and truths, and rejected Him.

In *Matthew 16:20*, He charged His disciples not to preach anymore that He was the Christ, or Messiah. The Jews, in their unbelief, had rejected Him and His offer to establish the Kingdom.

In the next verse, He began to prepare the apostles' minds for His soon-coming death on the cross. As the Jewish leaders became more hostile and vocal concerning their plan to kill Him, the crowds of those who were brave enough to be seen openly in His meetings became smaller and smaller.

Being human, the apostles began to doubt and question His leadership. Peter, as their spokesman, was provoked to come right out and ask Jesus, *"Behold, we have forsaken* (left) *all, and followed thee;* ***what shall we have therefore?*** *" (Matt. 19:27).*

Jesus calmly answered them that their paycheck for all of their sacrificial service was to rule the earth in the coming 1000 year Kingdom (*Matt. 19:28-29).*

Luke gave the plainest statement of Jesus' teaching about the Kingdom to the apostles in *Luke 22:29-30.* Jesus promised them, *"And I appoint unto you a kingdom, as my Father hath appointed unto me; That ye may* ***eat and drink at my table in my kingdom****, and sit on thrones judging the twelve tribes of Israel."*

Through the stress and unexpected events (His crucifixion) that followed shortly afterward, this promise seemed to have escaped the apostles.

Upon His resurrection, Jesus spent the **last forty days** of His ministry, before going back to Heaven, preaching and teaching about the coming Kingdom. Note this great truth as revealed in *Acts 1:3, "being seen of them forty days, and speaking of the things pertaining to the kingdom of God."*

This teaching concerning the coming Kingdom, where the twelve apostles would eat and drink at His table and sit upon thrones judging the twelve tribes of Israel, led the apostles to ask this question, *"Lord, wilt thou* ***at this time*** *restore again the kingdom to Israel?" (Acts 1:6).*

Jesus informed them that it was not for them to know **the times or seasons** (*Acts 1:7*). It wasn't the thing they should concern themselves with at that time. There were only two things that they were to be concerned about.

First, they were to wait in prayer and **be empowered by the Holy Spirit**.

Second, they were then to give themselves over fully **to spreading the Gospel to every creature** in Jerusalem, Judea, Samaria, and to the uttermost parts of the earth.

Jesus' exact comment to them was, *"**But ye shall receive power**, after that the Holy Ghost is come upon you: and **ye shall be witnesses** unto me both in Jerusalem, and in all Judea, and in Samaria, and unto the uttermost part of the earth" (Acts 1:8).*

Based on accomplishing these two simple commandments – being empowered by the Holy Spirit and then going out into all the world – He would fulfill His promise of **letting them help Him** rule the earth in the coming Kingdom.

That promise of being a king and sitting on one of the twelve thrones of Israel **hypnotized the apostles' minds** toward that future day and they never lost their focus. They constantly looked for the second coming of Jesus, which would usher in the Kingdom.

3. Work Toward The Kingdom To Come.

There were two things that were to be utmost on the apostles' minds as they led in their worldwide effort of evangelism. They were to be focused on getting the Gospel to every creature in the world, and on His coming back to establish His Kingdom.

They were to make a clear presentation of the plan of salvation to save lost sinners. They were to convince sinners of God's love and provision for every man. In doing so, they were warned that they would encounter hostility and possible death. On one occasion, Jesus told them that He was sending them as **lambs among wolves** (*Luke 10:3).* He was quick to assure them of His continual presence and protection. On another occasion, He said, *"I will never leave you nor forsake you."* On the final day of His earthly ministry, He literally assured them, *"I'll be with you perpetually, on every occasion until the close and consummation of the age" (Matt. 28:20).*

In the first major persecution against the church, Saul of Tarsus caused many of the members to be put in jail or put to death. When Saul was struck down in conviction on the road to Damascus, Jesus asked him, *"Saul, Saul, **why persecutest thou me?**" (Acts 9:4).* Paul was persecuting the Christians but Jesus was taking the treatment of His saints **as treatment to Himself personally**. That statement illustrates how close the fellowship was that Jesus and His followers enjoyed.

Jesus became even more connected and involved with His disciples **in times of danger** and persecution. When the man who had been crippled for 38 years was healed, the authorities became very hostile and threatening to the apostles. They brought John and Peter into court. As they observed the behavior and countenance of the two apostles, Jesus' presence seemed to shine through them. They took note and found, according to their standards, that the apostles were **ignorant and unlearned men**. Then the Bible says a strange thing, "*they took knowledge of them, **that they had been with Jesus**" (Acts 4:13).* In times of serious trouble, it seems that Jesus was with them to the extent that the authorities could tell it.

When Stephen was stoned to death, Heaven was opened and he could see Jesus looking down in concern. Then the Bible declares that the members of the council literally stared at the face of this dying man and *"saw his face as it had been the face of an angel" (Acts 6:15).* When Jesus promised his disciples, *"Lo, I will be with you always"(Matt. 28:20),* it was not an idle promise. One of God's children can expect Jesus to get in the fiery furnace with him as He did with the three Hebrew children so many years ago. The close, endearing and personal fellowship which Jesus gave His disciples in times of persecution and suffering is no doubt why **Paul desired the fellowship of His suffering**.

They were to get the message of hope concerning the sacrificial death of Jesus to every person regardless of **the personal pain and suffering** that they encountered. The salvation of sinners had cost Jesus His life. There was **never a more shameful** treatment of a human being than what Jesus suffered.

Why did He suffer? He suffered in order to save people from hell. On more than one occasion, He reminded the disciples that **the servant was not better than his master**. If He had given His all to get people saved, then He expected the same from them. They were to

work zealously until His return or until their death.

His coming meant rewards in the Kingdom. The second thing that was to be utmost in their minds was His imminent coming back to earth as the King.

As the apostles were saying goodbye to Jesus and staring up into the heavens where He had just disappeared, they were reassured by two angels who said, "*Why stand ye gazing up into heaven? This same Jesus, which is taken up from you into heaven,* ***shall so come in like manner*** *as ye have seen him go into heaven" (Acts 1:11).* How this experience must have burned in their memories and kept them **looking up for the rest of their lives**!

The night before His crucifixion Jesus gave them the promise that has blessed the whole world through the centuries. *"In my Father's house are many mansions: if it were not so, I would have told you. I go to prepare a place for you. And if I go and prepare a place for you,* ***I will come again****, and receive you unto myself; that where I am, there ye may be also" (John 14:2-30).*

This personal promise of His coming back for them, given on the last night of His life on the earth, must have always been prominent in their minds. They must have reasoned, "**If God created the Heavens and the earth in six days**, then just how long will it take Jesus to create some mansions?" How they must have treasured and been inspired by the final service with their precious friend and Savior and **the promise of His second coming**!

They would eat at His table. When He came back it meant they would have personal fellowship with Him and eat at His table. His personal promise to them was, *"That ye may eat and drink at my table in my kingdom..." (Luke 20:30).*

Can't you see how that promise kept them going in spite of their pain and suffering? They could always get up in the morning and say, "**This may be the day of His coming!**" As they faced martyrdom and watched their persecutors prepare for their executions, they could rejoice and say, "**This is the day!** I have won! I will get my throne and eat at Jesus' table for 1000 years!"

III. THEY WERE ASSURED OF ABSOLUTE SUCCESS

Not only did they have a perfect teacher who instructed them of the truths of God's perfect Word, they had **a perfect role model to follow and imitate**.

1. He Washed Their Feet.

By this simple act He demonstrated that they were to serve others. Paul amplified this principle when he wrote, *"Let nothing be done through strife or vainglory; but in lowliness of mind let each esteem other better than themselves. Look not every man on his own things, but every man also on the things of others" (Phil. 2:3-4).* As they imitated His servant leadership, it kept them from having conflict with each other.

2. Jesus' Example Of Humility.

Jesus was God but He took on the form of a man. As a man He humbled Himself, even to die on the cross, **the lowest act of self-abasement and humility that could be shown**. The Scripture states that because of the giving up of Himself to die on the cross, Jesus was given a name above every name and that all the world will **bow before him** and confess His Lordship.

The lesson the apostles learned was this. *"Let this mind be in you which was also in Christ Jesus" (Phil 2:5).* He that *"**will be chief** among you, let him **be your servant**" (Matt. 20:27).*

It is very clear by the example of Jesus that the ones who will be the greatest in the soon coming Kingdom will be the ones who humbled themselves in faithful execution of their service to Jesus, even if it meant death. All of the apostles died a martyr's death except John, who as an old man in his nineties, gave the world **the book of victories** called the Book of Revelation.

3. Those Personal Promises Transformed The Apostles

Examine the lives of the apostles before the resurrection of Christ and the empowering of the Holy Spirit. **They were scared, confused and disorganized**. They were even hiding behind locked doors. They had heard that Jesus was alive, but the fact hadn't become a reality yet. They also had been promised a future place of glory in the coming Kingdom, but they hadn't caught the impact of that promise either. **It was all just a bunch of words**. But forty days with Jesus and the empowering of the Holy Spirit transformed them into men **whose course could not be changed or stopped**.

Part of their power came from the infilling of the Holy Spirit. But great services such as the ones they experienced on and after the Day of Pentecost could only carry them so far. The promises concerning the future Kingdom could, and would, carry them all the way through their lives. If they endured hardships, then their positions would become even better because, *"If we suffer, we shall also reign with him" (2 Tim. 2:12).* The other promise states that the more one suffers, the greater the eternal glory will be. *"For our **light affliction**, which is but* *for a moment, worketh for us a far more exceeding and* ***eternal weight of glory"*** *(2 Cor. 4:17).*

If they were martyred then they would have their place in the future Kingdom **plus** the crown of life, which is one of the supreme rewards. *"I will give thee a crown of life" (Rev. 2:10).*

The apostles understood their jobs. They were to get the Gospel to every creature in the whole world regardless of their personal cost.

They understood their rewards, "to eat and drink at the Master's table" as they were ruling and reigning with King Jesus. **But little did they know** that parts of **that Holy City would be named in their honor** by their grateful Lord (*Rev. 21:14).*

4. They Traded What They Couldn't Keep.

The apostles, along with every person since Adam, couldn't keep their lives. They all died (except Enoch and Elijah). All of the millions of people since the apostles also have died, regardless of what they did to prolong their lives. The apostles knew they would die. It was only a matter of **when, how and for**

whom. They chose to give their lives for a **sure thing,** to obtain the promise of Jesus.

5. For Something They Could Not Lose.

The absolute promise of Jesus to the apostles, that if they gave their lives to get people saved then He would give them a throne and a position to eat and drink at His table during the 1000-year Kingdom, **transformed them**. They were raised from a small spot on the earth, working at nominal jobs, and elevated to one of the top positions in the millennial reign and eternal ages. They traded what they could not keep (their lives) for something they will never lose – **God's glory, commendation and eternal fellowship**.

They labored for Christ and His Kingdom and their reward will be exactly what they worked for and much, much more!

The possibilities of **your future abode** range from the huge mansion, which will be the headquarters of a city of honor and prestige, to **the humble shack of a servant**. This is the reason the Apostle Paul admonished his converts to *"work out your own salvation with fear and trembling" (Phil. 2:12).*

IV. THE COMING KINGDOM WAS THE GREATEST MOTIVATING FORCE IN CHURCH GROWTH

1. Forty Days Of Intense Training.

When Jesus arose from the dead, He used the saturating principle to train and motivate His apostles – *"being seen of them forty days, and speaking of the things pertaining to the kingdom of God" (Acts 1:3).*

Jesus only had forty days to inspire and train the apostles so they would get the Gospel to every person in their generation.

How Could He Do It?

Please consider – He needed to major on principles that were simple and would capture their minds to fearless service for the rest of their lives. May we suggest some of the principles that He may have pounded into their minds?

* They were created in God's image and likeness, and through His power they had great potential as His ambassadors (*Gen 1:26).*

* Man was originally created to have dominion, or rule, over the earth – *"and let them have dominion over..." (Gen. 1:26).* Just Adam's failure did not change God's eternal purpose for creating man.

* David restated man's purpose in *Psalms 8:6, "Thou makest him to have dominion over the works of thy hands; thou hast put all things under his feet."*

* Jesus taught that everyone, who by faith overcame and *"keepeth my works unto the end, to him will I give power* (authority) *over the nations" (Rev. 2:26).*

* He told them that He would return at any time, so to watch at all times for His coming.

* He explained their jobs to them very clearly. They were to be empowered by God's power, and not their own. They were to get the Gospel to every person in Jerusalem, Judea, Samaria, and to the uttermost parts of the world.

* He said that He was sending them out as lambs among wolves, but if they suffered with Him, they would also reign with Him. Based upon their complete daily effort in getting the Gospel to every creature, that when He came back they would eat and drink at His table for 1000 years as they served as kings over the twelve tribes of Israel.

2. Peter, Paul and James' Interpretations Of Jesus' Teaching Concerning The Kingdom.

We realize that Paul was seen by Jesus at a later time, but examine the teachings of these early believers.

The Apostle Peter, the first pastor of the first church, was able to lead the church to win and then disciple perhaps as many as 300,000 to 500,000 people in a five to seven year period. How did he get these people to forsake all and endure persecution as they worked and served Jesus? We believe the answer to this question is that he was able to take their minds off their present problems of life and give them a long range purpose, by teaching them about the soon-coming 1000-year Messianic Kingdom.

3. Future Glory Offered To Pastors.

1 Peter, Chapter 5 begins with Apostle Peter addressing the elders (pastors). In verse one, Peter told them he would personally be a *"partaker of the glory that shall be revealed,"* speaking of the coming Kingdom. Then he told the pastors that they too could "receive a crown of glory that fadeth not away," in *verse four*. In *verse ten*, he gave them the steps that the grace of God would enable them to share in Jesus' eternal glory.

They would have to:
First, avail themselves to God's grace;
Second, realize that they were called to share in His glory;
Third, go through the suffering and trials which would equip them to be mature, strong and settled leaders;
Fourth, wait until the Judgment Seat, where they would get their glorified bodies and receive their places of leadership in the Kingdom.

No doubt, Pastor Peter schooled his preacher boys and early leaders in **these steps to eternal glory** and future leadership.

4. The Kingdom And Glory Offered To All.

In the next book, the book of 2 Peter, the great pastor offered this glory to every born again Christian.

Peter's inspired promise is recorded in 2 Peter 1:11, where he stated, *"For so an entrance* (into the 1000-year Kingdom) *shall be ministered unto you **abundantly*** (with great fanfare) *into **the everlasting kingdom** of our Lord and Savior Jesus Christ."* This abundant entrance is offered to all who will build properly upon their true foundation, Jesus Christ.

In verse five, he admonished believers to add to their faith (personal faith in Christ as their Savior) virtue (good habits or works). Then, in order, he gave them six other principles which they were to add into their Christian life and practices. They are:

Knowledge (Biblical knowledge)
Temperance (Self-control)
Patience (Steadfastness)
Godliness (God-likeness - Piety)
Brotherly Kindness (to all men)
Charity (Godly Love)

Peter told the early disciples that if they were zealous in performing these Christ-like works, then they would have tremendous honor and attention bestowed upon them as their King rewards them when they enter into the Kingdom.

He got their minds off this world and onto eternal things. He gave them goals to strive for in pointing them to the Kingdom. He gave them things to work and suffer for in order to achieve eternal rewards and glory.

Peter was a perfect example of someone who **lived in the world**, but was **not of the world**. He lived for Jesus and His coming "well done" in the Kingdom to come.

His teaching on the coming Kingdom must have given the early disciples an understanding of what the Christian life and work was all about.

They lived their lives in the light of eternity.

They understood what the Christian life was.

They performed the Christian life and works.

And, because of this, **they spread the Gospel** throughout the known world.

5. The Secret of Paul's Great Ministry.

Whereas Peter inspired the first church and led them to saturate the city of Jerusalem with their doctrine *(Acts 5:28)*, there was one man who stood head and shoulders above any other missionary in spreading the Word of God throughout the world. The man? Paul.

Paul won and trained masses. Much of the book of Acts reveals his exploits, while fourteen of the New Testament books reveal his teachings and passion. There have been few men who have had such singleness of purpose and who were so driven by their love and obedience to Christ. Almost everyone in his generation was impacted in some way by this great warrior; through his preaching, his pen, or through those he had personally won. In some way, Paul's life touched and influenced his generation.

His greatest accomplishments were in training and motivation. One can examine the great accomplishments of his ministry.

The church in Ephesus. It was here, within three years, that he and his missionary team of ten preachers were able to win and disciple enough Christians so that all in Asia heard the Word of the Lord, both Jew and Greek. Tens of thousands were saved.

d. His ministry as a prisoner in the city of Rome. One of Paul's greatest burdens was to preach to and win Roman soldiers so they would carry the Gospel, not only home to their Roman citizens, but to the vast areas where the Romans ruled the world. Handcuffed to Roman guards while a prisoner, Paul won and discipled hundreds of the choice members of Caesar's guard. The Gospel spread to Caesar's household as well *(Phil.4:22)*, and Paul comforted the members of the Philippian church by saying that his imprisonment **was for the furtherance** of the Gospel *(Phil. 1:12)*.

Although these two accomplishments were more than most men ever accomplish in an entire ministry, neither represent his greatest work through a local church.

e. The crowning jewel of his ministry. The church that shines like a spotlight in a dark night is the church at Thessalonica. It was one of Paul's shortest mission works, **about three or four weeks** long, and he testified that he worked night and day while there.

Paul said that this church became an example to all the believers in Macedonia and Achaia *(Thess. 1:7)*. In addition to that, the whole Christian world had heard of this zealous, committed church *(verse 8)*.

The people of the church had turned to God from idols **to wait (earnestly looking)** for Jesus from Heaven. In fact, there are five chapters in the first Epistle to the Thessalonians. All five of them end in reference to the second coming of Christ.

*"...**wait for his Son** from heaven"(I Thess. 1:10). "...in the presence of our Lord Jesus Christ **at his coming**" (1 Thess. 2:19).*
*"...**at the coming** of our Lord Jesus Christ" (1 Thess. 3:13).*
*"...remain unto the **coming of the Lord**" (1 Thess. 4:15).*
*"...be preserved blameless **unto the coming** of our Lord Jesus Christ" (1 Thess. 5:23).*

The second coming of Christ ushers in the 1000-year reign of Christ. The disciples' minds and hearts were fixed on the future coming Kingdom and they were convinced it could and would happen at any time.

In the second chapter, Paul was revealing his love and effort to develop them into dedicated, strong Christians who would walk worthy of the Name of Christ.

Paul reminded them that he was gentle among them when they were first saved, **as a nurse to children** *(verse 7)*.

He also told them that he not only risked his life to get them saved, but would give his life for them because **they were so dear to him** *(verse 8)*.

He reminded them of his behavior while he worked with them and for them. His lifestyle was **holy, just and unblameable** *(verses 9 and 10)*.

In verse 11, he said that he exhorted (encouraged), comforted and charged them, **as a father** would exhort, comfort and charge his own children.

Now all of this is tremendous; and, no doubt, if these things were the only things Paul did for his converts in Thessalonica, they would have been a good church.

But verse 12 is the key to their greatness. Paul revealed to them and convinced them why he was demanding so much of them. He explained to them, probably over and over again, why he was **working night and day** for their good. He wanted them to walk worthy of God, so they would hear **God's "well done"** at the Judgment.

Paul's exact words for working so hard and suffering so much in order to develop the people of this great church are found in verse 12. He said, *"That ye would walk worthy of God"*.

Then he explained what so few of God's children understand. Please note what Paul taught, **which transformed the members** of the Thessalonian church.

"...God, who hath called you unto ***his kingdom and glory****"(verse 12).* They understood that although they were **in the world**, they were **not of the world system**. Their King was coming back, and it could happen at any moment. And then **they would share in His Kingdom and glory**.

Some may question that the preaching was not about the immediate coming of Jesus to establish His personal Kingdom, but that He was using the word "kingdom" in the general sense of the word. The unsaved Jews who heard Paul preach were so stirred by his teaching that they caused a riot. The mob brought Jason and some of Paul's workers to the authorities and lodged this complaint, *"These that have turned the world upside down are come hither also; Whom Jason hath received: and these all do contrary to the decrees of Caesar, saying that* ***there is another king, one Jesus****" (Acts 17:6-7).*

Paul was promising every Christian who took a stand and was winning souls a special place in the soon-coming Kingdom. They would serve 1000 years under King Jesus.

Paul's hard work, prayers, examples, tears and teaching paid off as this church shined as the crowning jewel of this humble man's life and ministry.

6. James, The Second Pastor Of The Church.

Add James' testimony to the teaching of these two giants, Peter and Paul, and you will be able to comprehend the zeal and devotion of their converts.

James said, *"Hearken, my beloved brethren, Hath not God chosen the poor of this world rich in faith, and* ***heirs of the kingdom*** *which he hath promised to them that love him?" (James 2:5).* "Heirs of the kingdom" wasn't a phrase that James used to give his members a warm and fuzzy feeling. It was the promise that Jesus used often to get the early saints' **minds off of the world** and to motivate them to give their lives in devoted service.

We have seen the teaching on the imminent coming of the Lord and His Kingdom by the three most influential leaders of that day. They had many of their members looking for Jesus to come in their lifetime. Their lives were fully given to meeting their coming King and hearing Him say, "Well done, thou good and faithful servant. Enter into the joy of thy Lord."

This conviction and their total devotion to Christ led them to evangelize their generation. Now these three spiritual giants are resting in Heaven, waiting for their future positions in **the soon-coming Kingdom**.

Everything Rises Or Falls On Leadership

Motivation of leadership is the key to church growth. What greater motivation to pastors than to hear their blessed Lord say, "**Well done. Come and help me rule the earth for 1000 years**".

NOTES

NOTES

NOTES

NOTES

NOTES

NOTES